Telling
Things

—

Telling Things

poems by

MICHAEL J. ROSEN

HARCOURT BRACE & COMPANY

New York
San Diego
London

Requests for permission to make copies of any part of the work should be mailed to: Permissions Department, Harcourt Brace & Company, 6277 Sea Harbor Drive, Orlando, Florida 32887-6777.

Library of Congress Cataloging-in-Publication Data.
Rosen, Michael J., 1954–
    Telling things: poems/by Michael J. Rosen.—1st ed.
        p.   cm.
    ISBN 0-15-100240-1
    I. Title.
    PS3568.O769T4   1997
    811'.54—dc20   96-28800

Text set in Walbaum
Designed by Geri Davis
Printed in the United States of America
First edition
A B C D E

Acknowledgments

The author would like to thank the National Endowment for the Arts and the Ohio Arts Council for the fellowships during which some of the included poems were written, as well as the editors of the following magazines where these poems—several in earlier forms—first appeared:

The Boston Review / "Fountain"
Carolina Quarterly / "Ocean City, October"
Chicago Review / "Walden Pond"
Cincinnati Poetry Review / "The Reader Falls Asleep in His Library"
High Plains Literary Review / "Small Consolations".
The Journal / "Unseasonable Warmth" (under the title " 'Palpable and Mute' ")
Kenyon Review / "Groundwork: A New House"
Michigan Quarterly Review / "Chattel"
The New Criterion / "In Rousseau's Jungles" / "Window Washing"
The New England Review/Bread Loaf Quarterly / "Trying to Write You a Poem on Our Anniversary While Downstairs You Roughhouse with the Dogs"
The New Republic / "Videnda"
The Paris Review / "Refrigerium"
Salmagundi / "His Father Phones with an Idea for a Poem" / "The Night Before His Parents' First Trip to Europe, His Mother Writes a Letter" (also anthologized in *Best American Poetry*, 1995)
Seneca Review / "Thoreau's House Site"
Shenandoah / "The Inheritance" / "A Guide to the Old World" / "The Map of Emotions" (also published as the winner of the Poetry Society of America's Gustav Davidson Prize)
Slow Dancer (U.K.) / "One Reading of the Situation"
Southwest Review / "Pilgrim Signs"
The Threepenny Review / "Blue Tail, Green Thumb, White Lie" / "The new neighbors who rent next door, their laundry"
Western Humanities Review / "Snow Scene with Two Dogs" / "Cenotaph"
Wigwag / "Watching Fireworks on the Statehouse Lawn"
The Yale Review / "Always the Deeper Meaning" / "The Growing Conditions"

Contents

for Mark, who tells me things

Telling
Things

———

Early Work

Your two heirs apparent tussling in back,
we descend the limestone path to the home
where both your father and you were born.
Beneath the van's wheels, gravel resows
itself among itself, revising our visit
with all that's come and gone, been lost or buried.

Inside, you write our morning's itinerary,
each an emergency number, while I befriend
the latest in a succession of family collies
(the one that will belong to *your* children's
memory) who waits in the driveway for each return.
That's when I discover your name among the stones,

a syllable inscribed on a porcelain shard,
surely the broken foot of a simple vessel.
Like learning a word that suddenly appears—
and just as suddenly is everywhere—
the bits of pottery divulge themselves,
each a glint of meaning underfoot.

Hand-painted details, the celadon lip
of a lidded jar, crazed and lustered salts,
your penciled script in cobalt underglaze—
the collie pads across these blunted chips,
oblivious as generations of wheels,
and I find nothing to approach an explanation

among the handfuls of these artifacts
I recognize from the childish Age of Clay,
the not-so-ancient college years we'd shared.
When you rejoin me with your father, the pieces
briefly reassemble into logic:
long after you'd moved away, at your insistence

that there was nothing of your early work,
nothing from their basement, you wanted saved,
your father reclaimed the pottery, throwing each ware
against the concrete steps, then casting it all
unceremoniously across the drive,
another layer of the sudden and gaudy past.

In the picture window, Grandma and the kids wave
good-bye. Your father restrains the collie. We board
the van, so cavernous and quiet now
I can hear—or so I tell myself as we make
another version of the drive—the little
breakages that tell *someone was here*.

GROUNDWORK

Chattel

Four years from now
what will be the difference between land and stock
at least as it applies to us? Moving in, a labor?
Each year's accumulations are like years themselves,
convinced the time we share is all divisible by things.

How will we budge:
a Parsons table that could sleep two uncomfortably;
a headboard of glass blocks—even less heavy loads...
the lesser things, that like anything we hold, will be held
against us; the ivy cuttings that grew to be the view?

Willed to the next tenant:
housings for *our* bibelots, the bouts of matching
     swatches,
floors hand-sanded the color of sand, the summer you
     spent
painting along eighty panes of double doors and—
how you measured!—a mile and a quarter of trim.

Built to be lost:
fitted draperies, couch (recoverable?), all the comfort
familiarity affords, the still lifes (a perpetual
donation of the season), the arbitrary order
of drawers that governed nonetheless.

Glad to be rid of:
the ceilings' need for spackling (our seasonal white lies),
the plaster dropped like states from a puzzle,
    unrelenting
wrong numbers for Somebody's Autobody, the mind-of-
    its-own
garage door, the tiresome drive for any missing
    ingredient.

Already good as packed:
tubes of prints we've meant to frame, years of
    magazines,
clothes good for one last season, the library
(already stored in memory, with its two subjects:
This I have read; This I keep meaning to).

Unchanged by our stay:
the still-sealed cartons of previous subscriptions,
belongings, or so we call them, as though with
    cardboard boxes
we might yet master them . . . Either we always have
to move, or have no need to. We've nothing to claim

as chattel, besides each other
and these personal effects so eager to leave us behind.

The Inheritance

At the heart of the yard's enormous ash
(a tree that could support anyone's wish
for lineage), inside a rotten V that splits
the living from the dead limbs,
we found a stranded fence post
of heavy iron and heavier rust—
another bit of unexpected chattel
that came with the sale
like the other wooden trunk in the attic's
too-small-to-crawl space, packed
with stories, abandoned, estranged,
and now, somehow, to be related...

The ash exceeds this new ring
of our arms' link
(broken as we reach for one another),
a girth begun when the orphaned acre
was plotted a century ago, or before,
when the seedling enforced a line
connecting—disconnecting?—neighbors
in what hoped to be a neighborhood.

Surveying the long-untended grounds,
we can imagine the sapling bound,
then bent, beside the metal, opened
by it, and driving upward, dividing
itself equally on either side
of the fence as though to reconcile
something the neighbors themselves could not.

Once the remaining fence had gone—
hacked down? raised again? rerouted?—
the post in the thickening ash was set
as resolutely as the pin
in your now-buried father's hip
(for if there is homology,
a bone is most like a tree),
at last, bent toward healing itself,
conceding the settlement of human rifts.

The post protruded, at first, an onus,
a yearly trial of its owners
—new ones, surely, by then—
like a sword in stone,
slowly swallowed to the hilt,
scar and wound swallowed, too, and who and what
might have grown beneath its story.

Whether for persons or trees,
years are all we ask of a surgeon;
ours offered the quick succession
of dry rot, ash borer, the unpredicted
drop of decade-thick, dead wood,
a brittleness wind could wield against us,
or, alternately, cords of hard, slow-burning ash,
to last beyond our single deed
and the fires of our current residence.

The new neighbors who rent next door, their laundry

drip-dries in the rain. The sad fact is
for six days their whites have hung in downpours,
drizzles, and intermittent moments of sun—
the narrow yard pinned with diaper squares,
bath towels, bedclothes, and boxy underwear.
Although their drenched spirits did lift a bit,
giving up a little weight to the wind,
the load continued to sag lower and wearier
as if the very thought of human contact
was more than it—or anyone—could bear.

(Officially, we've never introduced ourselves,
but it's easy to fit our own reluctant figures
into those blanks, our dreams across those sheets.)

Just when the longest articles threaten to scuff
the bare ground where, if it weren't this sodden,
children would be winging through the sun-
soaked fabrics, their faces veiled and unveiled
behind the white and shivery bafflements,
the bathrobed mother dashes into the rain
to the tree that juts through our common fence
and tightens the lines attached to a half-dead,
overhanging limb of a mulberry
we've been meaning and meaning to remove.

(The family of five makes do or does
without another day. Just how much
would it take to cart it all to a laundromat?)

There must be one close by? Closer by,
we thought and thought of offering ours—the dryer
thrown in at the title closing (the timer's
erratic; AIR, DELICATE, WASH 'N' WEAR
are all the same to it; the screen extracts
such lint our clothes should be translucent),
and then we did, we made the offer in person.
In *reality*, all of our exchanges
strained through their screen door, the mother
moored by children around her legs and arms

as if, at any second, a gust might raise them
above this weather, beyond the embarrassment
that was so clear we *had* become transparent

(naked, despite our wealth of dry, warm changes).

The Growing Conditions

The garden in the group-home yard
was dug long after spring departed
and since the late, lanky starts
were planted, has not been touched.

A load of dirt was dumped, a swatch
of turf removed, and someone—an aide,
a relative godsend—
created the bed on a passing whim.

The residents' days (for what my study
reveals) are spent entirely, expectantly
pacing our block and the next as though
change were just around the corner

like fall and the first frost, or chain-
smoking in a row of rusted chairs
that surrounds the garden; provident
or powerless, they watch the plot:

cracked, pithy turnips and beets
choke in a snarl of bindweed,
accusatory bolts of lettuce
signal above a strangulation

of tomato vines and fruitless squash,
scorched cauliflower, rotten—
a total ruin. Meanwhile, dollies
of Veg-all ascend the ramp to the kitchen.

There's one woman, whose name always
fails me, who comes to our garden gate,
admiring all that's managed to grow
in light of our excess of trees,

summers of drought, and a soil of clay.
When finally I come to settle
the riled retrievers, who likewise fail
to recognize her, she requests

a prized flower for her boyfriend.
(*Demands,* really—though etiquette
would hardly diminish the wince of the cut.
But would this garden's worth of costly

mail-order perennials
that disappoint in ways I won't
compare to children who have grown
without, or even despite, love—

would that suffice? Or would my wish,
somehow fulfilled, for "constant color
throughout the season," or a surfeit
of blooms in this broken shade save me

from selfishness? *Un*begrudging
kindness—can it alter lives
beyond our own?) Morning and night,
like Phaëthon dragged behind a brace

of golden dogs I cannot or will not
train to heel (I've tired of trying),
we wend a wide, erratic course
around an overgrowing world.

Groundwork:
The New House

———

The tree service commissioned months ago
arrives the morning of the first snow,
both unannounced. Less the season's
gift than its wrapping,
a thin, translucent tissue holds
whatever presents we might imagine
possessing, for example, a bank
of lily bulbs, dormant since our move,
now frozen solid and safe
from the impact of this morning's work.

In a rotted box elder we're told is nothing
but trouble, a garbage tree, a man is guyed,
cradled among the crooks of dead limbs, steadied
by spurs kicked in the trunk, and still he sways
unspiderlike, climbs without a cat's agility,
clings less confidently than a squirrel.
He works the way we might imagine
a man works in a tree,
while it is the tree we can't imagine
brought within the hour to the ground.

How graceful the simple extension
of his hand, a wand that merely parts,
pauses between branch and trunk, then passes
as though the tree had prepared for this,
knew, the way each node possesses
that layer between twig and stem,
to yield at an appointed season.
And what quick work a man of forty makes
of one box elder coincidentally,
he tells us, forty-odd years of age.

Were the man to fall his would be
unlike a spider's, though the eye can drop
his body and pose it: the tree's marionette.
Nor would he fall like the stubborn cat
borne so often down the neighbor's ladder,
nor like the squirrels who jump from our roof
routinely shy of a just-now-severed branch.
A man would fall the way a tree falls,
a thud already imagined beneath my feet,
as the floor absorbs each felled segment.

Around the man, an aureole of sawdust arches
in the cold December sun, a snow more brilliant
than the ordinary flakes that continue to fall,
more kin to the color of the sun itself,
as though the tree in its last
relinquishing, descended in gold leaf,
the foil of a man-made heaven.
And this, so incidentally, while the man,
certainly an artisan of sorts,
was looking elsewhere, for anything but signs.

Nor did I, calling you to the window,
expect this coarse annunciation
in which a man works without the knowledge
that he's appointed or accused,
and if either, then for what or by whom.
But now the eye, assigned, opens
onto the adventitious scene.
The other windows reveal
a blond boy of six, the man's son,
whose curling bangs have framed

the pure blush of his exposed cheeks
in the blossom of a hooded parka
the azure blue of a Byzantine mantle.
He has climbed commensurately high,
and, straddling the garden gate, showers
giddy handfuls of the wooden flakes
over our bounding puppy, a golden lab
so much the color of the heartwood
that his appearance, ecstatic in this,
his own first snow, must be an attribute.

Before the man descends
what's left of the trunk and levels it
to the ground upon which you and I
have—perhaps too casually—imagined
all our ends met, he fastens
his rope at the blunt top and crowns
the sheered and crooked stake himself,
a temporary, human ornament
placed above the gilt scatterings
of all that's fallen before him.

Window Washing

Close as any embrace, we press together—
you, on a ladder tipped against the house,
me, crouched inside the kitchen sink—
twelve mullioned panes within our grasp.

We wave at—in truth, *against*—each other,
in patterns the weathered casements circumscribe,
like all the other greetings and departures
they've witnessed, within their manageable squares.

Yet blurry gestures aren't what we read,
nor what their insulated touch confers
as we settle on one unyielding spot,
but the grim opacity of grime, Windex,

and webs, streaked like ambiguity
between us. Oh, and you, of course, must scan
(a second time?) the random sheet from the morning
edition, wadded behind your clenching hand.

Whatever incident your side reports,
my own opposing view insists, "No Reason-
able Offer Will Be Refused," illustrated
with a waterbed that grants untroubled sleep.

Finally, there's tapping, a finger's accusation,
a smudge someone must own. More smearing, mist
and scratching...until we see the fault, if it must
be someone's, is the rain's, acid-etched

like habit on the glass. Next comes the instant
when the eyes shift from the wiping hand, from the bled
and sodden news, to the bright unblemished glass,
bedazzled by the sudden reflection there:

the mulberry I should have let you fell,
the marble countertops you knew I'd stain.
Another glance replaces this, when the glass
conducts our gazes like incidents of light,

and our heads, tilting, doubting their eyes, perhaps,
survey the glints of sun. But that perfection
breaks, breaking as we say the sun breaks
among clouds, when the window allows the eye

to dissolve the glass and its little solipsisms,
and to see beyond it, as though our furious swipes
had been at nothing, at shade or at air, at some
foreseen inclemency, at something behind,

and not between us, where, now, one face is framed
between the draperies we couldn't afford
and one, among the vines of unnamed ivies.
So satisfied, before the next set,

there is one other glance the eyes catch
—at least, my eye caught yours—when the cleansed
    window
permits a look that is, just as we start
our small descents, adoring, inside and out.

TELLING THINGS

Trying to Write You a Poem on Our Anniversary While Downstairs You Roughhouse with the Dogs

With a vocabulary of imitations,
baby talk, and song, you, dear, give voice
to everything: the door, linoleum,
a treat . . . gradually, the house itself
(at least its lower orders) assumes the secret
language of conspiracy—celebration,

rather, of simply coming inside, of simply
being companions who have conceded more
than a little boyishness, more than a little
doggishness, to the other unknowable side.
But save a word or two I *can* distinguish,
the roughhousing, the house itself, encodes

your exclamations (not unlike our own
affection's ever-changing long- and shorthand)
in patterns of stops and starts, scraping nails,
whoops, dead silences, and barks
that might communicate for all you know.
I don't know. It's hard to ignore, harder

still to attend, yet sometimes I've discerned
news that's news to me in your doggerel
and double-talk (for you must answer, too)
and voices that I recognize as yours
and yet you've never used with me. I see:
the key to the code is that it won't be cracked

or reconciled in poems—what I hear,
conveyed through wall vents, conducted up the stairs,
is how we always must sound to dogs: tones
divorced from the particular, a *now*
followed by other *nows,* with nothing like
our proud and inconsistent details confusing

the issue—which is always trust, isn't it?
whether we betray it or not, call it
love or not, or any other word
(or words—or lack of words) to justify
the way we want to feel and behave and seem
to construe a world given to disaffection.

Now: laughter leaps two stairs at a time,
an unmistakable word *Michael* that means
"Let's go see Michael." Ahead by a nose,
the dogs skid into the room and nudge my hands
from their devotion, whether or not they see it
as that, or understand the broken silence.

Always the Deeper Meaning

Again this morning, and probably all month,
our house quakes steadily as your heart
that sleeps, somehow, through the chthonic beat.
Too intimate, the tabletop and plate
are monitors; the floor and lamp take up
the sympathetic pulse as though what
we dreamed or dreaded were merely out of sync
with our insouciant fates, and I were forced
to face your sleep as the perilous thing
it is, making its nightly reparations.

Outside is the simplest of answers: a pile driver
advancing down the city's major artery.
Blocking all traffic, it roots a course
to China, or hell—whatever unfathomable
sense resides below the surface wreck.
Along with six decades of asphalt, years
of implausible patchwork, gravel, and brick,
the pounding hours have unearthed our bodies
(buried so loosely beneath the summer sheets)
and fears momentum usually puts to rest.

This is a version of hell dredged to mind:
a vigilance where the inanimate
conducts the coursings of your heart,
the window shudders regardless of its view,
the tremorous paper underlines the news
once thought removed. Either you'll wake,
disowning the mock echo, or the crew will reach
that final bed, bind the site in orange,
and route the vehicles past the implacable scar...
but wait. It's stopped. Again, this morning.

Snow Scene with Two Dogs

Warm enough for snow to fall, for us
to fulfill a neglected promise to the dogs
that, oddly, we keep between us, we walk
to a park where opaque white has covered the world
of their concerns, which, blissfully and because
of us, are none—except for the two of us.

There's little we envy in their abandon that skirts
the field (of *vision:* we can't be out of their sights)
or in the democracy with which they trouble
a field so perfectly primed by the heavy snowfall
that where they slide, what they paw or nose,
is scumbled from matte white into whitish hues,

newish elements in the self-conscious
(I have contributed that) genre scene:
"Two Dogs in Snow, with Lost Scarf,
Fallen Sign (VACATION BIBLE SCHOOL),
Arching Brambles..." (tangled in their coats,
no doubt), "...and Patrons" (obligatory tributes,

crude likenesses of quilted figures
all but cropped out of the dogs' picture).
And though it's joy to witness a joy invoked
by *Walk?*, a simple suggestion, it hasn't worked
for us. It probably shouldn't. We wouldn't dream
of addressing one another (or the problem,

well, somewhere in the field) with shared commands
like *Speak!, Shake! Leave it! Understand?*,
or, more to the point we've been missing, *Heal!*,
an imperative. We're trainable. We're here—
that's something—but what's immediate is, we're
    needed:
the dogs have snow packed tight between their pads.

Sit, we direct them, *we'll help you.* And,
with the simplicity of obedience,
we *do* help, prying from the nerve center
inside each paw, from the equivalent
of our hand's palm, a huge pearl of ice
that's opalescent, almost, as it shines.

What *is* enviable, I'll grant them, is how
even this act—it's only their second snow,
compared to what is our sixth season this fall—
this the dogs redeem into ritual:
as each frozen pearl is freed, they feel
the need to seize it and chew it, wagging their tails

as if the very sources of pain were treats.
Good boys, we say, and then because it's
something to do, we fasten their leashes again.
The chill factor has waxed, the snowfall, waned,
as we recross the field we've muddied toward home.
Since then, I've thought of saying, my pet, let's swallow

whatever it is, but frankly, I'm not able
to find the reward, the moral of the fable.

Small Consolations

Our fingers dart among the burdened limbs,
pure exclamations, hardly completing a sentence
between us. As though we didn't have all the time
in the world, as though ripeness were a moment's
    notice,
we sample half the grove before settling
on a tree so laden with cherries, so low,
nothing seems out of reach.

Steadily the baskets fill with conversation.
We're only silenced with cherries in our mouths,
a taste we find insatiable, a sweetness
we won't entrust to memory. Given the ladder,
given the fruit seems denser above us, one climbs
higher, the other strays from this festoon
to its shadow's deeper red,

to an even darker shade beyond. In no time,
a word is tossed that someone isn't there
to catch. When I find you, bright like a tangled kite
within the boughs, our talking wanders on to
childhood trees, and again, caught up
in the hands' relay, the uneasy stretch across
the synapse of limbs, we're several trees apart,
in rows separated

by something inconsolable, a distance beyond
a voice, or the good one's words might do for the other.
The silence accumulates with the mounds of cherries,
uncalled for and clear as the juice the hours
have leached. How is it one desire leads
in all directions? That first tree held enough
to fill the afternoon.

When it occurs to us to stop, we've picked
between us more than we might can—or
in a month, consume: a rash trunkful of rubies.
We smuggle the spoils from the orchard like some
happiness we must deserve, but still
distrust. How rich we are that we won't save them,
that nothing we say need last.

Refrigerium

Because distance becomes tumescent in the heat
the haze erases buildings out of walking range.
We've managed to walk as far as the backyard
and spread a quilt there, one huge book the three
of us hold open, just as our own fingers hold
our separate texts. Lemon slices, sugar, and ice;
shake until the cubes melt and bruise the rinds...
we downed the pitchers in minutes, refilling the leftover
party cups half a dozen times. Now,
absently conjugating verbs that end in *o-i-r,*
you fish out every lemon and nibble at the implacable
pulp, setting the sections among the shady grass
like phases of a lunar calendar for the world
our quilt describes. "Tonight the meteorologist
says to watch for Jupiter, just left of the moon."
(The *moon*? So, you'll have it reassembled by then?)
Out of the same nowhere from which the planet will come
you announce that. Oh, let the lemons lie there,
upended yellow boats, their empty hulls
so clean and white, let them always ferry
such heaven-sent distractions from ourselves.

A Moment's Claim

Conceding the dogs their routine morning walk,
I come upon you unexpectedly,
midstreet, spellbound, standing where the bus stops,
in the city's excavation of burgundy bricks,
asphalt shards, and crumbled limestone curbs.

The dogs immediately defect to join you,
rejoicing as though you were a rarity—
it *has* been hours—they'd just unearthed themselves.
Here, you tell me, right here where you stand
no one has stood for nearly a century.

You guide me through the strata so reverently
it seems you've dug this shallow, man-sized pit
and that it's nurtured our grafted family tree.
Yet what I find is how much more you've found:
a civilization before our house was built.

(*Our?* Note how shallow my sense of history?)
Their family intact, the dogs elect to walk;
but me, even more than my desire
to occupy this recovered ground with you,
I want to leave you here, still unexpected,

enraptured, beside yourself with discovery—
this breakthrough from the other side of the world,
if worlds are what must separate two men.
The dogs conduct me around the familiar corner.
Less permanent an artifact, we two

will reach a milestone, turn a decade's corner
soon, a date we've paved and patched with extra-
ordinary compositions such as walks.
Until I do lose sight of you, or you
decide you've had your fill, it's ten and not

a hundred years I see, it's love for you,
alone and transported, and not your moment's
claim on a place soon to be sealed with tar
so that the bus, recklessly turning the corner
(just now), can carry you away again.

One Reading of the Situation

So indecisive, the sun is overworked,
the air soggy, and the whole effect ruined
but not as quickly dismissed as that "I-hope-
you're-happy-now" remark of yours, which the current
of events has taken up, tossing our boat
with the usual velleity of waves.

Anchored nearby, a sailboat attempts a reading:
its mast wavers among the possible
predictions: *Fair . . . Clearing . . . Precipitation.*
But what it gauges, the future of some
hazardous part of nature, is speculation
we'd undertake if it were cooler. Right now,

it's not, and the water's not, though the single
motion of your dive, from lounge chair to lake,
implied some kind of known relief—not
to me, St. Francis at the transom, reading
above the water's undiscipled edge.
You swim around the boat, clockwise—

like clockwork or that oblivion
of instinct that stations the heron at the bank.
Below the inches of water, your tan blends
with the greened bronze of the lake. The blue stripes
of your suit, a serviceable gift from me,
keep you from further conversions. Too late:

You don't hear me shout, *"Watch! watch! watch!"*
when a catfish bobs, belly-up, in reach.
And the heron—blue-gray among blue-gray roots—
seems to abide you, swimming there, in harm's
inevitable way. As reluctant to suffer
metaphors as the fisherman trawling the shore

who casts his lines to the boles' entanglements,
or those leaning trees that will become the lake,
or the lake which, now, the city wants to drain,
the heron shirks my preachy observations,
like beaded water, with one wide wing stroke.
We can cause one to fly but not to stay.

Your swim reworks our argument; but doesn't
repetition turn to metaphor,
tenses replaced as though nothing
had yet happened, or everything might still?
In today's version, the exercise goes round
in circles and time passes on a stopwatch—

so it isn't later after all.
"Had enough?" I ask as you flop aboard,
startling the heron to flight. Well, something did.
Its cry is likewise startling, and so
raucous that, even if it's unrelated,
it jeers at us and our attachments.

Unseasonable Warmth

Could we make something of the alchemical sun,
other than tea and weekend escape plans,
its change would be as obvious to humans
as to tomatoes: our sprays of cherry and plum,
the exuberant burgeon of Big Boys—all that green
a better nature than ours has given up on.

Outside, with our half-read, about-to-be-thrown-
out paper (all month we've been prepared for autumn,
to grin and bear it indoors till May) we happened
to glean some real advice: "How to Ripen
Tomatoes in Their Own Gas," preserving the season
in "breathing" newsprint. We took the suggestion

literally, took that very section
and swaddled the stunted fruits of our labors in
the delivered world of Sunday, October 10,
where the expected high is eighty-one,
and a front of clouds moves east in our direction.
Smug with a dream of like successes, we're open

to what greater uses we might assign
our stacks of fire-hazardous subscriptions,
*The Monthly This, The Annual of That, American
Whatever:* Ripen our stash of juvenile wine?
Expose our slides of silhouetted Cannes?
Sequester each small misgiving that still remains

between us, beseeching, childless, orphaned?
Larger issues, of public—global—proportion,
we could consign to Christo's veilings: Commission,
for instance, a wrapped and splintered political chasm...
That wayward, well-meant dream has stalled since then.
Agreed, the fruit was slicable and reddened,

but the wrinkled headlines squinted back: predictions
keeping their words, the stale and timeworn
stories of how nothing's new on earth, just green-
as-ever death cropping up in barren
plots. What will change those yellow, or soon-
to-yellow, bitter truths into reasons

we can stomach? In what can we seal those columns
of type? In crosswalks, lobbies, bank lines, trains,
the total strangers we've met—and also been—
have one refrain: "Can you believe this sun?"
Wrapped up in that one prevailing condition,
there's hope that it could mean, not simply be.

Often we find the sky drawn and halved
a blank, a line like a horizon lifted
ruling the cirro- cumulo- nimbo- fracto-
(God knows!) clouds
into now and about-an-hour-from-now
. . . we they
. . . fair foul
(and even the foul into cats and dogs):
some temporary troubling watershed.
Actually it's a decorous cold war
that tempts us with such easy allegiances
warring fronts that blow hot or cold
and in any case will dissipate
midday into the muddled currents
that reign benign— admit it, *benightedly*
over our vicissitudes our middle ground.
A lone example: the day we put the dog
out of its misery we minted our own;
crossed the time-honored borders of pain
others' ours.
But just as death did not remove the dog
from his appointment on the ottoman
by the stoop my side of the bed
(as we did his collar, leash, and bowl)
we are not so easily led from guilt
to guiltlessness lulled from sleeplessness
to sleep. For what is spirit save a body
absence makes motions the arms adopt
the heat of memory where sorrow warms itself
a voice—one's own? that solitude befriends:
our practical refusal to give form up
to entropies like grief. Now expectation

wags its tail at the door heels at the corner
dodges among our feet. The world the dead
inherit like anyone divided from us
is this one: Here and the beyond are waged
under one immortal impassible sky
(What difference if the *im* is snipped from each?)
where, every day, we count or is it cut?
our losses, take or is it give? our readings.

A Thirteenth Sign

Although this storm has yielded to traffic and plows,
our nearby athletic field, locked for good
it seems, upholds the season and the gates allow
a diorama of winter the neighborhood
can conjure amid wind chill and slush while we trudge
between sealed houses and the curbside hedge
whose streetwise face is salted and grayed from its
     station
of having witnessed—destiny, not destination.

As always, the lone players from the home team
(to judge from prints the ice has fossilized
some other man with dogs has similar dreams),
the retrievers and I chart a ground they've revised
month after month as though it were a heaven
of scented stars, that snow, just for a season,
reveals to us lesser creatures ("lesser" for deigning
to think that seeing is all, that having seen

provides all further predictions). Off-lead,
the dog stars commence their pan-athelon:
touchdowns, home runs, citywide records for speed.
They bound, tackle, and dodge . . . now and then
accepting a word from their plodding downfield coach.
The other man's prints—a crescent arch,
a zodiac of pinpoint stars—are criss-
crossed with dog tracks: the snakes of a caduceus.

I step into his steps: Although our strides
don't match, his course fairly predicts my fate.
The dogs do sniff the paw prints petrified
here—snow remembers scent far more than weight—
or hope, for that matter. "Hey! Who was here?
In *our* field!" I ask them, expecting an answer
but, as though snowblind in the olfactory
sense, I cannot obtain the dogs' story.

Streetside, amid the stampede of soles, I find
those other boots and paws, lose the trail
at one corner, locate it again as we wind
toward separate lives. How could I have failed,
when that constellation turned into our yard,
to recognize your tread, when you and I, the untoward
gods our two dogs love, marked thirteen years
today? Surprise: that's what our stars declare.

VIDENDA

His Father Phones
with an Idea for a Poem

———

"At the cemetery, placing a canning jar
of those silver-leafed flowers you seeded
beside the privets, the ones with the purple stalks,
I noticed—it's sage? You mean the cooking herb? . . .
Your grandmother never used it, I don't think—

I figured they were just flower flowers.
The bees adored them—as well as yours truly
for bringing them. Remember the bees during
the eulogy: those slow, undaunted ones? . . .
Yes, that's right, one stung you on the wrist.

But in the stone—this is the part I thought
you might—well, you decide: Within the words
chiseled across the granite, this dirt,
this baked-on clay, had sealed half the '9' in
'1890,' all the 'y' in 'Mary.'

At first I guess it's something a car had flung
from the road, some kid scraped off his shoe,
but inside it was tunneled, cluttered with white
egg sacks, and a pair of writhing wasps I'd gouged
prying the hardened chunk with my house key.

Mud daubers' nests . . . Yes, there were others.
They seem to pick more English than Hebrew words,
Aunt Eva's had a pair. And Dr. Lantz . . .
Isn't that the sort of thing you use?
I'd be happy to go with you if you want."

The father's son has never viewed the nests,
just as he's never visited the grave again
and won't, until it bears another's name.
But the son has seen (at least, he presupposes
he has so he can forego such a poem)

what the site has meant to the father, and so,
in the son's mind, the father stands in its place,
stands as though at his mother's grave with that
unlikely bouquet of sage, this likely idea
for a poem the son, were he inclined, could write.

This makes the son as poet suspect the father
attends most any image—even graven—
waiting just as a ram attended the father
of Isaac, readied for the substitution.
He smiles at the irony his father

probably sensed—oh, life and death,
the larvae hatching from the very words
that claim a woman, a generation, for earth.
Perhaps the father considered (for now, the son
provides him these lines) the way the dirt

obliterated the name, erased it—or started to,
anyway, before his return—eased it
into forgetfulness (a pain too
like remembrance), as if the mud daubers
were sent by Time, healer of wounds in flesh

and mud and stone, where, one day, won't they
all be likewise, otherwise, engraved?
He might have recalled the words that struck his son
—why, the father couldn't say—their last
time together in temple, the prayer that ended

"May God destroy Death forever and ever."
Perhaps the father had seen how one could say
the wasps were vanquishing death in their seasonal,
personified, albeit primitive way,
and, come to think of it, how his son might try

comparing that with his father's minor, impromptu
destruction of the clay defacing the grave.
The son invents too much for the father, who has,
in fairness, read all his verses, admired their talent
to grant a son of his such happiness.

Notebook after notebook inherits the verse
that isn't written; more distant relatives
billet the mud daubers' returning broods;
and the father succumbs to no less mortal failings
than the next man—for instance, the one

in an adjacent bed, whose heart valves
babble with his in a language as clear as mud.
What moves the mother to tears moves the son
to poetry (or so the mother's tacit
understanding runs), though all have wept

at further complications they've been spared.
The son has spent the hour writing by his father,
in a chilly room where hybrid zinnias
he brought are blossoming on shortened stems.
The father wonders if writing is for the son

what prayer has been for him, although the son
is only grading exams, and prayer, he'd raise
his eyes were the father to ask, is any form
that holds an excess—pain or love—until
we can accept we've given it away.

Years later, though it needn't have been,
the son thinks of the poem—he isn't cooking,
although that might have worked; he isn't brooding,
yet that frequents, too—as he dodges the bees
in the hedge at his parents' house, gathering sage

to deck the garage with upside-down bouquets,
to then perennially forget, leaving
the father to pitch them, dried, into the trash.
What to do with an herb as potent as a symbol
whose slightest presence disturbs the whole of what

has gone before or will come after, as urgent
as if some "I" would call to "you" across
these distanced lines. "Sage," the son begins
again, sacrificing another image
beneath the few daubed words he keeps alive.

The Map of Emotions

A popular version is simple to construct:
We're driving cross-country, the map is spread
across our laps, the dash; it nearly obstructs—
it has become the view. An unpredicted
wrong turn, and we successfully skirt ANGER,
smack into the eye of SCORN, and coast onward,
sighting the meridian of REMORSE. There's danger
both in looking back and looking forward.
The children voice in the rearview mirror
a tacit part of us (they've found PERSISTENCE):
"Where's the SURPRISE?" We promised; we won't forget.
We'd rather cross the line into INDIFFERENCE
than spend the day basking on the isle of REGRET,
always a favorite resort this time of year.

According to the map, the seas are quite severe
(those whitecaps are surely larger than life-
boats); as for the land, it's either still
to be discovered or, discovered, was left
behind for others to claim and have their fill.
The ships foundering in the Left Hemisphere
chart the regions of APATHY and DESPAIR,
channels that empty, though empty without end,
into one unsounded doom. But the sails (*Compare!*)
in the Right are trim with LOVE and its warming trends:
PRIDE, WONDER, and AWE. But how do the boats
repair from one into the other realm?
And where do the two worlds converge, that moat
of brackish ambivalence, mercuric, overwhelmed?

Alas, no legend accompanies the chart.
Moorings, anchors, oars—they're all worthless,
for where among the vessels of the heart
is there a place that won't return us, much less,
where we will not return? What one current
has sunk, will surface, upwelling somehow.
Why trouble with a map, if everything's current?
"CHARTED 1626"—now
tell me the little-known world's not been revised
since then, and isn't again, each time we trade
positions, taking a nap or the steering wheel.
"Land, ho!" the kids exclaim through their handmade
telescopes (tunnels of fingers)—a whale,
more likely: that way we all can be surprised.

Further Notice:
For a Friend at Sixty

Who was it said that time has been invented
so everything won't happen all at once?
(Not remembering hasn't prevented
a single ounce of full-grown impatience.)

Years are nothing more or less than yearnings,
pretending that our course from A.M. to P.M.
is longer lasting, a fatter indulgence, burning
eternally in limbo. *Carpe diem.*

It's only recall, that brutish referee,
that separates this waging happenstance
into before and after, arbitrary
corners. *Time out?* Not a chance,

since in the long division of light-years
aren't we but a moot, minute remainder
of one imperfect age (that disappears
before it answers even the closest star)?

Then what is sixty but the present address
of where the traveling light of one's attention
has been absorbed so far? *Here,* for instance.
Oh that the sun would never reach the horizon,

ever lengthening the shadow of days
until we are so long in ourselves that there is
nowhere we haven't happened, no other phase
to shade this moment's ever shining notice.

For My Brother at Thirty

Thoreau's House Site

Except for gravel roads, each circled T
labeling the trails, and paths worn in the ground
like something memorized then handed down,
all a hundred years have added are unlikely
things that help reclaim the site for history,
little allotments set aside for loss:

Imagine the cabin fit within the stand
of concrete stumps; meals cooked above
this engraved plinth; and someone to speak
the passages carved into wooden signs.
What these recall, the trees cannot record.
It's far easier to feel the presence

of an afternoon of pilgrims. By now their visits
must total more than his two years, two months.
Of late, a mound of stones is being compiled
(initialed, pocket-size, spray-painted,
still others immobile as the hearthstone)
like evidence against time. Soon

enough the cairn will tower above the cabin—
higher than we suppose the cabin stood.
The area is cleared of all but bark
and pebbles that waves of feet have all but worn
to sand. We're nearly at the pond
before we pass a stone worth bringing back.

WALDEN POND

This is where you swam, abandoned, all summer,
a pond the eyes' glance will contain, the lungs'
capacity. Few stones, new-fallen boughs,
schools of minnows skittish as premonitions,
the water is clear to where the feet hang free
and light gives out and goes green.

You beat your own course to a familiar cove
but I can't swim without stopping to judge
how far we've come, how far we've come apart,
gauging with clouds and a periphery of trees
too distant to show progress. What is it
I expect (a dead fish, kelp, a log—your leg)

to stop me like a pool's side, fractioning
the surface into small accomplishments?
It's akin to fear, this trust that insists
there is nothing here. Already at the inlet
two boys are casting, their bobbers trolling
between us. So the pond does provide

accordingly: catfish and carp; absence.
It's a second immeasurable swim back
to the towels tied on the overhanging limb.

VIDENDA

Wherever you've driven us, spun from a rotary
into one historic background or another
(Revere's house, North Bridge, the authors' cemetery),
all I have focused on is two brothers
posed against—well, blocking—a battlefield,
a worn memorial. You: always defying
a guard or gravity, your face concealed
in variable expressions. Me: I'm trying
not to notice, then not to show I do.
The self-timer clicks like a disap-
proving tongue. Months, miles, the old breach
between us advances another frame. SCENIC VIEW
AHEAD. What can it matter if, this trip,
we just forgo the Common, or Singing Beach?

Ocean City, October

We pass the last guard station
(farther than we feel like walking back)
and a few families collecting shells
four months of families overlooked
then bought (more polished versions)
from shops that seem like shells
themselves just now, abandoned.

Small as seed pearls on an abacus
sailboats slide along the horizon ...
a gain to the right ... then back for a loss ...
in the end it seems to come out even. It's odd
how the boats fall off the edge of the world
disproving our view: one moment buoyed like the sun
which sets the next moment, leaving us chilled.

All we count are three fishermen, their lines
cast up at clouds—ah, now we see,
at three laughing gulls that lurch past, climb,
then stall like kites. Clearly the men have had
no luck. And small wonder. There isn't a tackle box
in sight, or bait, or a bucket to hold
whatever it is they catch with only patience.

Then why are the gulls stalling? Between the poles
and the pull of rising tides, we continue
to walk, ducking lines we have to imagine.

A Guide to the Old World

Our travel agent has packages to offer
and trouble listening to where we want to visit.
Really, we don't know (that's why we phoned)
but it isn't "Continental Sampler,"
"European Mosaic," or "Exquisite
Contrasts of East and West." "Nothing simpler?"
we repeat, "Can't you station us in Rome?"

The agent argues—actually, vouchsafes:
"The Old World won't always be preserved.
Let's face it, Europe's a nuclear firing range."
So that's the deal, the value-packed escape:
low fares to our worst fears; observe
the ancient ruins before a modern mishap,
an incentive like a good rate of exchange.

The charter brochures descend. (We were forewarned.)
The agent insists on being our guide; his captions,
translating each scene of our travelogue,
are blazoned through the Swiss alpenhorns;
rumored in Keukenhof among the factions
of bulbs; rising in the Salzburger Nockerln.
We see the model tourists toasting "so long"

to new friends, and suppose, just as they
have finished their demitasses and aren't there now
to welcome us, likewise Les Invalides
out of focus behind them. The Passion Play,
we hear, will close at Oberammergau,
their agreement breached before Judgment Day.
On every tour, the exotic's guaranteed,

yet nothing is far off as history: of the unforeseen,
which will become it first? Each fated
map is emptied of all but ports, each coast of
all but harbors, its countries allied with schemes
of color and occupied by planes—antiquated
shadows of planes, as large as Liechtenstein
or Andorra would be or those nearly ghosted

countries we can remember inexactly.
Each airplane's wake is thicker than a boundary,
each one a conclusion drawn matter-of-factly.

Cenotaph

For years there was only the hometown paper, the lone
vending machine set like a cornerstone
at busy crosswalks, outside strip malls.
And now, just like downtown itself—marble
facades to staunch each inner-city disease—
a skyline of newspaper storeys
(self-serve, coin-op, Day-Glo bins of paper)
has intervened among the vast skyscrapers,
as if our journalists had tried to model
a city according to late-breaking, final-
edition, human-interest afterthought.
The Wall, The Beacon, Dealer, Post, Report,
and *Blade* (and last, in line, the brimming *Trash*)
reality's dispensed: your choice of harsh.
Today, *Thursday, June 28,*
1990, a verified Goliath
among these waist-high, tabloid monuments,
one of the homeless who works the downtown
    pavement—
cardboard boxes, winter coat, bicycle,
whose home, let's say, developers recycled—
is banging door-to-door, shaking the foundation
of each—hometown, state, and nation—
in hopes of one slim outcome: a dislodged
quarter, some lost and significant change.

In Rousseau's Jungles

In retrospect, what should we make of
the labored-over faces, features
that appeared to fit (like pieces
from childhood's idyllic puzzles),

or predators benignly traced
from the encyclopedia's plates,
who crop up in the succession
of houseplants that furnish your tropics?

Favorite leaves would germinate
whole species of unforeseeable
symmetry—memory will do that,
sentimental, unforgiving

medium. Their fronds and leaflets turn,
not toward the sun—that ripest orange
which blazes yet won't light up a thing—
but toward us onlookers.

And what of the domestic pets
figuring too largely or too little?
Where do water lilies grow well
with cacti; Indians—*New World!*—wrestle apes?

(You wrestled with that black shape
yourself.) What was too hard to recall—
how things customarily recede
(roads, rivers, a distant vista),

how things are logically grounded
(roots, foreshortened feet)—you skirted
by growing grasses, lengthening hems,
elaborating on the better known.

So badly outflanked by the flora,
one vaguely feline menace clamped
on its vaguely cervine meal, is less
threatening than boughs of boa constrictors,

burgeoning banana chandeliers,
strategically positioned spikes.
Though grass sabers and fences of reed
prevent any thought of escape,

we are, to be perfectly candid,
elsewhere, posing our private fears.
Could the cultivated really
overtake us? We're on- and off-

lookers, not unlike you,
rendering our own habitat
with only memory's thoughtful fumblings
to dictate what goes well with what,

and who, overwhelmingly reduced
to a figurine in the foreground,
should keep a place in the under-
story from being overgrown.

Fountain

Penning
another draft, the lines run
dry, well before the mention
of death. The point
dipped into the ink's
reserve, the pen
drew its own conclusion,
filled like any syringe
rushing its contents
to the source of pain.
How to shunt
the flow for the present,
to turn the pen back into a pen,
to keep an-
other object from having
its fill of you.

in memory, F. T.

Green Thumb,
Blue Tail, White Lie

———

Pausing at every flower as though rapture
alone could pollinate your garden plot,
you lead me among the dense tropical beds
of species I recognize, if at all,
from produce displays, insipid houseplants.
How far afield from the Ohio we shared.

You've taken root yourself, naturalized
as the papaya's prodigal seedlings potted
for any willing guest. Hibiscus hedges,
persimmon, penstemon, ornamental lime,
arbors of jasmine, pools of hyacinths, palms...
the only missing attraction you drove me to see:

a 2000-year-old live oak,
huge as a deity, that encompassed us
in the convolutions of its arms, bare
but for a raiment of resurrection ferns,
and welcomed our names upon its uncarved trunk,
a palimpsest of those it has and will

outlive. Amid this nomenclature flashed
a quicksilver, blue-tailed *lizard*?
anole? a native you'd never seen before.
Searching among the underbrush, you rose
disheartened, unaware that on your sleeve
the vanished iridescent *gecko*? clung:

ebony striped with yellow, the length of your hand,
an all-too-vital thrumming at the throat,
and that arresting tail—azure, sapphire,
the color of innocence, could we see that spectrum.
It's only now, today, that time, or time's
imagined itinerary, stands still

while you conduct the complying creature along
your arms and neck...to pose atop your thumb...
deliver its message at your ear...descend...
but then, as if we'd tacitly agreed
on something, suddenly needed a conduit
for lost or merely longed-for tenderness,

you clasped my hand to prod your discovery,
despite my reluctance, across our suspended bridge.
A few moments of harmless proof, of almost
imperceptible tread, and the *chameleon*?
jumped, but not before I sensed its meaning.
Meanings, rather—unnamed and uninvited

and each attached like news of mortality
(what's new is how we sustain our ignorance)
to anything whose lifetime is shy of
the human span of want: the turning fruit,
a graying dog who claims my rooms, the haste
with which beloved ecstasy is spent.

Meaning, the virus that has found your blood,
this even less known creature you lastly revealed
while on this garden tour, has seized the hours
we shared as though to prove (in poetry's queer
culturing), there is no future that does not hold us
in contempt: We are meant to be history,

despite the white lies with which we bless
our time-consuming acts. (The *hours* shared!
So what of days I know nothing about?)
Meaning: meaning is much too profligate
to trust the cuttings we tender one another—
imaginary species pressed between

the chapters of an unread book. Which means,
you sent me home with bay leaves, spongy strips
of cork-tree bark, a pouch of dried persimmons,
and now, a postcard arrives to finally name
the demon: *"Southeastern Blue-Tailed Skink."*
So I have seen it. And you. And the live oak.

A Letter, for Micheal

However far in the years-at-a-glance
I manage to postpone, and so prolong,
your death, yours is imminent ("so long"
is time's single, consoling utterance),

only because, among its wealth of other
opportunisms, it has acquired a name—
letters, anyway, in acronym
to make it easier to say not suffer.

For all the hopes of health, longevity,
empowerments, cures (read: miracle),
there does remain the matter of your will,
a physical thing with more posterity

than poems, in which we friends, a web of family
you wove and rewove as a spider fashions
its lair, absorb your life, scatter your passions
(all that in our meted years will not be

ash), and bear the name you—years ago—
altered as though to change your genetic code
from male to immortal, like a child
that refuses, despite such love, to grow.

One week our talk's confined to two dimensions—
the future of the art you've lived among
(mirrors that never show you aged or young);
the next, your stories of each artist's intentions;

then what of your own work, your pupils, costumes...
For everything, we hazard a suitable shape—
a catalog, gallery, videotape—
your spirit might temporarily assume.

    [The same nothing that forestalls your death
    forestalls these thoughts—no matter that empathy
    is all that occupies the difference. Like zeros,
    words increase nothing when multiplied.]

Another week's most fitful dream described
all this to me: I am bequeathed the volumes
—poems, stories, pictures—that pranked your rooms.
A quirky pantheon, each book's inscribed

to you, the pilgrim of a universe
that shares only your name as common cause,
and the varied prints' and scripts' perceptible pause
as they approached the vowels you reversed.

Save that most self-conscious transposition,
your boxes merge within my library
as if the alphabetic order could bury
grief as well. Here's what the dream envisioned:

I choose a book my eyes, my memory cells
(already feigning loss despite my age)
have never known, and yet its title page
recalls me *friend, beloved, dearest Micheal,*

and cites the reasons for such deep esteem,
respect, or gratitude. There is a date
as well, a city I doubt I can even locate,
and there, there, imagination seems

unable to continue. Without you, I mean.
But then, as if I could pretend to read
the future (at least the one I must concede
myself), I do go on, continue to dream.

I open each of your volumes, break the spell,
add a proofing mark within each *Micheal*,
and so transpose your name, again, annul
the sequence, make you, not mine, but mortal.

Watching Fireworks
on the Statehouse Lawn

Lawn chairs unfolded in the left-turn lanes,
children crouched in pajamas on the car hoods,
five tiers of legs festooning the parking garage:
by dusk, half the city has converged to watch
the man-made firmament, explosions that open
overhead like spokes of a 200-year-old
umbrella (all show and no protection).
Around us, the mirrored buildings flash
as if set off by sparks, the air shudders,
the grass flinches, and within our chests, a pounding
our hearts know only from exhaustion or fear.

The dogs alone will not be comforted,
shivering behind the tires. Their better instincts
must reach beyond our giddy childhood, far back
to some unappeasable storm of cannon fire
or strafing, to a threat we scarcely recognized
in the sole misfiring, seven years ago,
that showered the crowd along the esplanade.

If only we were higher—in the rented
helicopters that are touring the site
like sequined ponies—or higher, so we could view
the fifty states as neighboring lots,
families with cherry bombs and bottle rockets,
or higher still, as one backyard, fistfuls
of glitter tossed (why not?) like fates to the wind.

But here on the ground the traffic takes hours
to untangle, the police directing cars
as though home were somewhere they assigned.
Above our headlights, the spent finale disperses
toward the suburbs. Gray, ecstatic ghosts,
each report nearly overshadows
the one before, just as on our radio
(Poland, Nicaragua, now Chad,
now local news: *rain before morning*).
The faint display continues as though well
out of earshot meant out of harm's way.

The Night Before His Parents'
First Trip to Europe His Mother
Writes a Letter "To Our Children"

On the envelope, her lone instruction
is boldface, all caps: **DO NOT OPEN.**
He pictures, inside, the slanting hand that penned
their minor news each week he lived abroad.

And yet beyond a list of policies,
securities, and keys, the words his mother
confessed she agonized over the eve of departure,
are inadmissible as joint untimely deaths.

This scene of composition, so inexplicable—
his mother, sleepless at the kitchen table
addressing her children from the other side
of tragedy, phoning to say, "I'd be too embarrassed

if you read it; I'm no writer like you"—
this scene obscures what work the son has done.
As if, in that unlikeliest event, his grief
would want a poem from her! Words to critique,

revise into some pretense of posterity!
If only his own work could seal such feeling
in an envelope someone might hold, hold dear,
but never open, exposing its words to light.

Two weeks the letter rests on the unset
table, holding his parents' place in the house
until their return, when the letter disappears,
replaced by snapshots stamped *Oct 90.*

These the children share around the table,
proving their parents had gone, at last, to Europe,
happier at fifty-nine and sixty-one
than they can remember. Next trip—their dates

are set, the planes and time-shares booked—
they will be farther, longer, and no safer,
leaving behind that or a different letter
to route the rest of our untraveled lives.

PILGRIM SIGNS

Pilgrim Signs

To show we've been there, journeyed, witnessed, praised,
returned, we bear these modern effects, descendants
of medallions—enshrined Madonna, John's head
upon a charger, Catherine with sword or wheel—
that pilgrims purchased half a millennium ago
at distant shrines to prove their faith and feat.
But ours are minted more from inadvertence
(alas, at no less a cost), cast
in substances less permanent than lead,
and worn without the benefit of blessing.

La Cucina Americano

Of the *porcini* mushrooms, *pecorino,*
the *pane integrale,* customs states
it clearest: What's not preserved won't make the trip.
To every dish reconstructed by memory
and substitution (anise instead of *finocchio,*
which stinks, the cashier says, like carp bait),
we add a measure of apology
(too much? too little?), that sympathetic salt.

Returning the Tapes

"Un poco tardi," quipped the librarian
working in Circulation. Shouldn't that
be *più?* er, rather, *molto.* It *has* been months
since our imperfect memorizations. Perfected:
the phrase, "Now, turn the cassette over, please,"
along with the international sound effects
of ocean liners blaring, a lighting match,
and clinking goblets of wine that introduced
the subjects we never managed to put in practice.

A POSTSCRIPT TO MICHELIN

On a train to Florence, idly skimming the last
of the endless guidebooks lugged along as though
history were mere connections—missed or made—
you find that, seconds ago!, just out our window!,
we passed the second oldest tree in Paris.
Overlooked it, looking ahead? That made
one thing, at least, we didn't mind
missing—and wouldn't mind missing next time.
This has become a standing joke for us.

RELIQUARY

And then there's our collection of arguable
vessels: *"In Paris it is the window; in Florence
it is the wall,"* amassed like artifacts
in the house of Sir John Soáne—models, molds,
engravings, fragments, lintels, busts, and urns,
proposing that an empire, after all,
is an arrangement of crafts—attached wherever
the eyes may find an idle space to light.
Whether or not we share his vision, we see
the rooms as he saw fit, forbidding change
at 13 Lincoln's Inn Fields.
How civilized to wonder—indeed, we fall
prey, too—just what the future will make of (or
take from) the ruins of our collected ruins.

PLAY OF LIGHT

Focused on singular details, we fixed
as well, uneditable fore- and backgrounds:
pop cans littering the portico,
taxis attending the Opera, a triple bank
of tourists (on, behind, and below each bench
encircling a fountain), irascible natives who crossed
our field, and even curious and heretofore—
or after—unseen aspects of our faces,
posed as if to prove the healthy dis-
regard such giddy travel offers us.

FURTHER ILLUMINATION

Here is a snapshot of a painting framed
within a larger, more recent painting.
In his addition, the later artist has shown
pilgrims whose prayers were answered by the inner
    canvas.
Yet what's apparent is five centuries
of lighting from tiers of votive candles have darkened
the central figure beyond mere chiaroscuro:
position is all that clues Her identity,
the Virgin, whose long miraculous work continues
in the successive version. The flash—unsooting,
but still, unsanctioned—of our Polaroid
appends a frame of its own, and so extends
our admiration to include a picture-
taking traveler and a shawled offerant,
bearing delphinium wrapped in that day's news.

POSTCARD:
ST. PAUL'S CATHEDRAL, DECEMBER 1940

Mounting 547 stairs
with nothing to view but steps turning from wood
to stone to iron, we rest at the Whispering Gallery,
that perfect drum below the huge rotunda,
that whispers everyone's word *whisper*
in both directions. There is no other secret.
No one will speak of the roiling pink-and-burnt-
orange sky of *December 1940,*
where the baldachino, like an act of creation,
prevails above the hand-tinted explosion,
which hangs in the nave, another altarpiece.
The conflagration of inks turns on a spit
of postcards, as well; on one of them we wrote
our house sitters (who saved the card for us):
"With skies like this, the two million tourists
who'll traipse through this year ought to be grateful
that all they've had to survive is gray rain
for the umpteenth day of their *petite vacance.*"
Our smugness, mercifully, has since moved on.

REPLICAS

In Westminster Abbey, we wedged our shoes
into the one-size-fits-all felt slippers,
and shuffled across the worn heraldic tiles,
our half-steps hushed—nearly hovering, as if
with everyone else, we were trying to sense
what being an angel—or just angelic—was like.
Once adjusted to an awkward, earthly gait
we gazed upon frescos so faint and flaked,
so eroded, it seemed the eyes had caused it.
Too late now, but couldn't something have been donned?
The damage *our* eyes did—to skim our journals,
hear our pedestrian tributes—was negligible.
Our visit is, itself, worn down,
burnished, like the brass headstones
we could have rubbed outside the admissions booth,
to a single anecdote by our retelling.

WAXING

We thought of buying huge indulgences
for one another, lighting them, then and there,
"for our respective retirements"—or packing a few
for some commemorative meal at home.
Rather, you sauntered off with a paraffin chunk
stamped in the tire-tread of your sandals: time
purchased from someone else's loved one's stay
in purgatory, prized free in Rome.

THE COMPANY WE'VE KEPT

Among our camera's takes, we're always slouched
against some great historic wall, shot
by the anonymous third party who knew
the Esperanto of the automatic-
focus, the phrase: "Here we are beside..."
Beside us? Strangers whose faces we meet each time
we rifle through the album, grown more
familiar than the landmarks we obscure.

COLLECTED STORIES

To the maze at Hampton Court, the water clock
by Covent Garden, the Raphael cartoons,
that shop with all the buttons made of horn,
or even the bistro where you left your first-
edition, secondhand Elizabeth Bowen—
we never returned. (Of course, it was no use
returning to the antiquarian bookseller
in hopes of a second, first edition.) We learned
our lesson, took it from that same Ms. Bowen
who wrote that repetition is the one
experience worth having. We do take pleasure
in our accumulating plans for "next time,"
that vague itinerary pen-and-penciled
in the margins of what keeps us here.

Snowdon Aviary

We added an easy dozen to our life list:
an Inca Tern, two Picazuro Pigeons,
a Straw-Necked Ibis, a White-Cheeked Turaco
—and the ever-present sparrows that flit
through every fence as if providing a size
for universal comparison. Searching for Gold-
en Pheasants amid the genuine grass and logs
that seemingly pass for habitat, we managed
to overlook the non-specific sparrows,
and saw clear through to the paired foreigners
at the opposite rail, hands shading their own
eye-ringed brows, leaning, likewise, toward us.
Nothing exotic there. Our focus drew back
into the foreground, as the day's—or years'—
list composed itself of memory's
rare birds: skittish, nearly extinct,
and each without a hope of progeny.

POSTCARD: *FLOWERS IN A TERRACOTTA VASE*,
JAN VAN HUYSUM, NATIONAL GALLERY

With perpetuity the only season,
the canvas attended its subject with a patron's,
a saint's, patience, its pigments wet enough
to act as water-changes in which the gifts
of providence sustain within a single vase:
from spring, narcissus; berries from June and July,
apples from autumn—and peaches and peonies
as each arrived in its prime.
                         Our reproduction
is pinned beside a window that frames our region's
flora: this week it's creeping honeysuckle
and a few limp sprigs that you've (barely) arranged
among the rearrangements here, in a vase
originally bought for your immigrant, ninetyish aunt
in the gift shop of our local *museo*.
Since returning (it's now been years, I admit),
we understand the vase is Florentine;
that, unbeknownst to us on our first trip
together, your aunt had died, her exact age—
untranslated since her one voyage—safe
in Europe with us; that weak solutions
of Sprite and aspirin extend the life
of cut flowers; and that it's not remembrance
but forgetting that yet commissions us.

The Reader Falls Asleep
in His Library

What happens next to Portia at the beach near Seale
is first obscured by the word *pelf;* now,
by his recalling how he stumbled on that aged
word for wealth at Jedburgh, reading aloud
Sir Walter Scott, and how it seized the treasured
contents of their rented car—and emptied it.
He lifts his eyes midsentence to shunt
the phrases from their determined passing
with—or without—him (just as a moment ago
his love pronounced his name, twice, in a slow,
inquiring voice, then let the question rest).
As if the ceiling's white were actually
the retina of that inward eye, the thought's

flash—wayward but yet detained—is focused
amid the traffic's capricious lights, leaks
in the unrepairable roof, and the other legible
subjects, risen on the heat of inspiration
and noted on that erasable slate. But, oh,
they're never collected, these temporary entries,
minute as homunculi, each a telling witness
that won't speak up. What "pelf" must know about him!
If only the unsympathetic things
attending us—matte, rough-hewn, unyielding—
were burnished by the wear of our persistence!
Then we could be held accountable by the gaze
of each accumulation, the glare of absent ones.

His eyes again surrender—accepting the plot
of turning pages, perhaps, as the soul must,
the plodding body after its nightly rounds—
to Portia, about to . . . to Eddie who has just . . .
But the book closes around his finger like a door
left ajar for someone supposed to return,
then slides from his lap, and seals his place inside.
While it could be a dream, the man is still
in his library. He is reaching for a book
the moment that, by a dreamy coincidence,
he reaches the middle of his destined life.
As when a god descends in peasant garb,
the man has no knowledge of the visit,

no time to start propitiatory measures,
and so he hesitates before his shelves.
The recently acquired, the obligatory,
those with stranded bookmarks: their titles,
like choices he could have suffered once, pass
beneath his eyes, academically,
and disappear. Now, what's left for him
to choose is part of an anthology
composed of all the books read and loved
in his half life—however poorly recalled.
Its first volume is waiting beside the sleeper;
the last—the very first book he remembers—
will occupy the final hours of his life.

Compressed among the pages' recounted facts
is proof of his endearing presence, distinct
as the folded corners, fingerprints, sand
blown into the binding, asterisks
that signalled some special passage, now vague
as a childhood monument that must have been razed—
though he never saw the wrecking ball, the vacant
lot, the fill. Here, too, like revisions
in the expanded version, are his own relations,
those with whom he has shared the stories, welcomed
among the ancestry of its centuries.
But he is the enduring theme, the one
who pours the tea into unrequitable

conversations at the drop-leaf table;
in his eyes, the settings are no one's properties,
no more than the daffodils near Grasmere
that five centuries of awe have tended,
visitors who rhyme the awaited occasion
with weddings, guidebooks, or loss. Here is
the passage from Wordsworth (reread at Grasmere)
where he took another roll of negatives:
the yellow horns along the unmarked roads,
announcing arrival, anticipating departure.
Where in Scotland did the waving bulbs relent?
Of all the pelf packed into the trunk,
the luggage, the heady plans for a second trip,

who wouldn't exchange it all for the daffodils?
He asked that of himself, his lifelong love,
and the couple in the backseat who held, with laughter's
perfect acoustics, his wrestled expressions of bliss.
Why couldn't he have stayed behind, and let
the first editions, the shortbread tins, the slides,
return home to conduct the ongoing neglect?
At the time, it seemed a question worth sharing.
As he wakes, whether or not it was a dream—
and if so, whether it will come true—
whether a meal was offered to a hungry peasant
or a god, he reaches for the fallen book
still waiting for him to follow, and calls

across (only the room) to the curled body
in the opposite chair, in another book's
other world, to his love who had kept a vigil
over his sleeping body as though it were
his place in the book that love, as well, could hold.
Those eyes meet his, acknowledging that he's awake,
and then resume their reading. Picking a page
that seems familiar, yet forgotten, frail
as a transcription of his dream, he begins it
for the second—or is it the third?—time, the one
beginning: *"Standing midway between*
these two distances, hands knotted
behind her back, Portia looked out to sea...."

"Early Work" is for Shirley Gromen.

"Refrigerium" is a place of cooling or respite, an ancient poetic form that is a song of respite to quench the burning souls in hell.

"Unseasonable Warmth" alludes to Archibald MacLeish's "Ars Poetica," in which he declares that a poem ought to be "palpable and mute / As a globed fruit" and "should not mean / But be."

"Fountain" is dedicated to the memory of Freyda Turkel.

"Green Thumb, Blue Tail, White Lie" is for Matthew Valiquette.

"A Letter, for Micheal" is dedicated to Micheal Milligan, 1953–1995.

"The Reader Falls Asleep in His Library," a prothalamion, was originally commissioned by Tom and Marian McCollough for Sharon Sachs and Donn Vickers. The book referred to is *The Death of the Heart* by Elizabeth Bowen.

ABOUT THE AUTHOR

Michael J. Rosen is the author, editor, or illustrator of some thirty books for both adults and children. His poetry has been collected in two other volumes, *A Drink at the Mirage* (Princeton University Press, 1985), and *Traveling in Notions: The Stories of Gordon Penn* (University of South Carolina Press, 1996). He holds an M.F.A. in poetry from Columbia University and has received several fellowships from the Ingram Merrill Foundation and Ohio Arts Council, as well as one from the National Endowment for the Arts.

Many of his efforts involve philanthropic anthologies to benefit Share Our Strength's fight against hunger, and humane efforts through a granting project he began in 1990, The Company of Animals Fund.

His many children's books, such as *A School for Pompey Walker, Bonesy and Isabel,* and *Elijah's Angel,* have received numerous distinguished citations, among them the National Jewish Book Award.

He lives with his family in his hometown of Columbus, Ohio, where he has served as literary director of The Thurber House since its inception in 1982.